NATIONAL GEOGRAPHIC

The Baby Shark

Sharon Street

This is a baby shark.

It has **eyes**
to help it see.

It has a **tail**
to help it swim.

It has **fins**
to help it swim.

It has **gills**
to help it breathe.

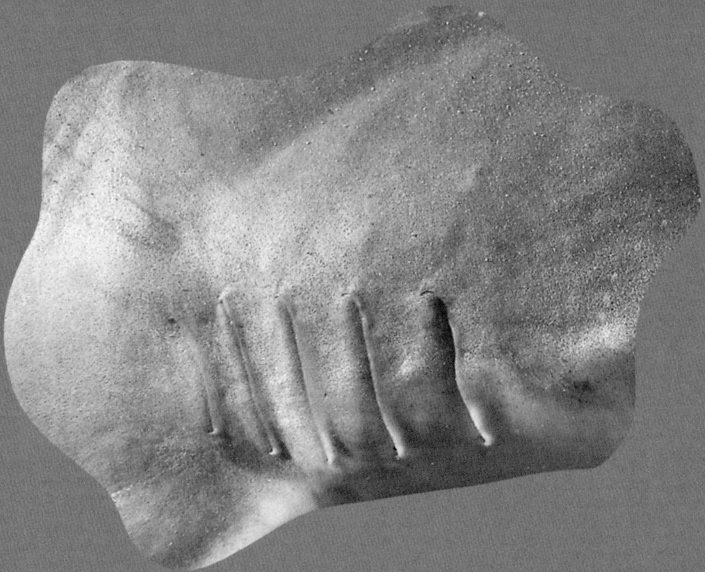

It has a **mouth**
to help it eat.

It will grow into a big shark.